Dear Amma

"Letters of Love, Laughter, Whispers,
Memories, and Everything In Between"

Dr. Vedavathi k Nandini

/ BookLeaf
Publishing
India | USA | UK

Made with ❤ on the BookLeaf Publishing Platform
www.bookleafpub.in
www.bookleafpub.com

Dedication

Dear Amma,

For your endless love, your patience, and your quiet guidance—thank you for being the heart that shaped mine. Every memory, every lesson, every laughter-filled moment with you lives in these pages.

To my little son, who reminded me of the magic of a mother's love and helped me see my own childhood through new eyes—this too is for you.

To all mothers, daughters, and those who carry love in their hearts—may these letters remind you of the bonds that connect us across time, space, and memory.

With all my love,
Your little word-weaver

Preface

Dear Reader,

Dear Amma is a collection of poems written as letters
from a daughter to her mother. Each one is a moment
caught in words—sometimes playful, sometimes tender,
sometimes sorrowful, and sometimes brimming with
laughter. Together, they weave a tapestry of emotions,
memories, and reflections that celebrate the
extraordinary bond between a mother and her child.

Through these poems, I invite you to step into the quiet,
joyful, and sometimes wistful world of a mother-
daughter relationship—the shared lessons, the unspoken
understanding, the laughter, and the moments that linger
long after they pass.

This book is for all who love, who have learned, or who
long for the presence of someone dear. May these letters
remind you of the timeless connections that live quietly,
powerfully, and forever in our hearts.

Acknowledgements

Dear Amma, dear readers, dear all,

I write this with a heart full of gratitude. Amma, for your love, guidance, and patience—thank you for every moment that inspired these words. Without you, these letters would never have found their voice.

To my little son, you showed me what a mother truly is and helped me relive every cherished memory of my own childhood with Amma. You brought those moments alive in my heart.

To my family and friends, thank you for encouraging me to write, to read, and to share. Your laughter, your listening, and your honest reflections have been my anchor.

To God, the Almighty—the unseen, mighty presence, the Mother of the universe—thank you for guiding me through every step of this journey.

And to the quiet muses, memories, and emotions that shape our lives, thank you for reminding me that even fleeting moments can become eternal when written from the heart.

With love and all my gratitude,
Your little word-weaver

1. The Mystical Bond

Dear Amma,

I wonder—
How did we happen to meet?

Did the Lord, the Almighty, decide
That we were made for each other?

Or... did you pray for a child
Exactly like me?

Or was it my penance—
To be gifted a mother as wonderful as you?

Or did Nature whisper secrets
And place us together in a basket of fate?

Or was it karma—
Reuniting two souls once again in this journey?

Or... was it our long-lasting wish—
To be inseparable souls,
Bound not just by birth,
But by something far older... and deeper?

Your loving
Daughter

2. My Teacher and Guru

Dear Amma,

Today I can write this letter
because you once held my tiny hand,
placed a chalk between my fingers,
and taught me to scribble on a slate—
watching the dancing words with pride.

I never wished you on Teacher's Day,
though you were my very first teacher—
the one who taught me to sing rhymes,
write A, B, C, D,
and count one, two, three.

I never wished you on Guru Purnima,
though you have been my greatest guru—
teaching me life's lessons,
guiding me through despair,
standing beside me like a pillar of strength.

You helped me secure good grades
and high ranks,
staying awake through long nights,

motivating me,
urging me to read that one last chapter
when I felt like giving up.

I don't know, Ma, if I have been
the student you hoped for.

But you are the best teacher I could ever have—
a light in my darkness,
a hand that never lets go,
a voice that shows me the way,
teaching me to choose the good over the bad.

Every rank, every success—
I owe it all to you.

Forever
your student

3. Come Home Soon

Dear Amma,
I came home from class today—
You had gone to see Granny.
But the house had forgotten to breathe.

There was pin-drop silence,
A hollow stillness—
deeper than death—
that haunted every room.

The house was spotless—
Curtains drawn, beds made—
But no voice asked me,
"How was your day?"

The fridge was full,
with food you'd prepared.
But there were no warm
hands to feed me.

Time was all mine—
to scroll through endless reels,
but I missed your gentle scolding:
"Enough now. Go and read."

It's strange, Amma—
how your presence
fills silence with warmth,and
 your absence echoes louder than words.

Come home soon, Amma.
This house has everything—
but without you in it,
it means nothing at all.

With love,
Your waiting child

4. Love Like Water

Dear Amma
"What is love?
How much do you love me?" I asked.

Amma—
love is like water:
a silent feeling,
divine,
never meant for showcasing.

It moves quietly,
a gentle act of kindness,
knowing what someone needs
before a word is spoken.

It speaks without words,
flowing through the eyes—
a single blink
carrying a million emotions.

It carries the power of satiety—
the quiet contentment
of knowing you never leave my side,
even when you dwell in heaven.

It is serenity,
a prayer
whispered between souls,
heard only by the heart.

Even before I held you in my arms
and our eyes met,
this current stirred awake within me—
shaping itself as life demands:
caring,
possessive,
overprotective,
guarding,
even anger and control.

But in every form it takes,
it is still love—
all of it,
for the one I love.

Mesmerized, I stood at your reply—
of water and love,
still rippling inside my heart,
your tender love echoing within.
Your ever-loving,
Love.

8

5. Deserving Break

Dear Amma,

I know you take pride
in being the most caring mom,
a loving wife,
an excellent homemaker.

You've poured your heart
into this family—
day after day,
for years uncounted.

But Amma...
please, take a break.

You wake with the sun,
brewing coffee for all—
yet forget to sip
one for yourself.

You polish every corner
till it gleams—

yet forget to see
your own glow in the mirror.

It's time now
to put yourself first.

Wear those vibrant sarees,
laugh with old friends,
watch a film,
munch on popcorn.

Go to a spa—
let the scent of jasmine
and gentle hands
soothe your soul.

And finally,
visit Granny's home.

Relive your childhood,
rest in her lap...
not as a wife,
not as a mother,
not as a homemaker—

just a daughter.
A child again.
You deserve it.

Your caring
Daughter

6. Flavours of Amma

Dear Amma,

Do you remember that evening last month,
on Papa's birthday, when we went out for dinner?
You loved the prawns tempura so much
that you walked into the kitchen
just to thank the cook.

That moment stayed with me—
it taught me how a few kind words
can lift someone's heart
and spark their brilliance.

It made me think of you, Amma,
and all the magic you've created in our home.

On rainy days,
crispy bajjis, simple dal rice,
and spicy chicken fry—
mmm... tastes like heaven.

On lazy holidays,
when mornings drift into afternoons,
the aroma of steaming biryani with cool raita
awakens every sleepy taste bud.

Crispy chaklis and soft, melt-in-the-mouth murukkus
are not just my favourites
but my friends' too—
the perfect snack on long road trips,
turning every mile into a celebration.

And Amma, your sweet pongal...
It is the definition of divinity.
The aroma of ghee,
just the right amount of sugar,
soft, mashed rice
crowned with roasted cashews and raisins—
mahaprasadam itself couldn't compare.

Even your bisibele bath is a masterpiece—
rice, dal, veggies,
all simmered gently with masalas,
flowing so smoothly
it needs no effort to swallow.

On dull evenings,
your strong coffee,
with a hint of milk and sugar,
feels like a gentle hug,
warming me from within.

Thank you, Amma,
for all the delicious dishes you've fed us,
for pouring your heart and soul
into every recipe—
even the ones you had to learn just for me.

I'm sorry, Amma.
All these years,
I didn't pause to savour the flavours,
nor did I see the tender love behind them.
I didn't thank you for your efforts,
your patience, your sacrifices.

Today, I do.
I thank God
for blessing me with you, Amma—
the best cook,
the warmest soul,
the flavour of home itself.

Your daughter,
savouring your flavours

7. More Than My Birthday

Dear Amma,

When October begins,
a soft bell starts to ring—
reminding you of a birthday
waiting at the month's end.

You remind Dad of the extra budget—
new clothes, sweets, and cakes so yummy!
You never let him forget,
not even once.

You wake me with warm hugs
and sacred blessings,
whispering to yourself,
"No scoldings today—it's her birthday."
And as my mischief blooms,
you tame your anger,
turning the day into sunlight.

You make my favorite dishes,
one by one,
feed me and smile
until my tummy is full.

16

You forget I'm grown-up now—
to you, I'm still your baby.
And Amma,
that love gives my heart a thrill.

At dusk, a party—
so simple, so sweet:
cake, snacks, songs,
and clapping to the beat.
All by yourself,
you make it so grand.
Amma,
there's magic in your hands.

And at night,
before the clock strikes eleven,
you whisper,
"Once you were in my womb,
kicking in heaven..."
You smile, you cry,
and hold me tight,
reliving your motherhood that night.

But Amma,
you forget one thing—
it's not just my birthday.

It's yours too.

The day you were reborn as a mother.

Happy birthday, dear Amma.

Forever,

Your little daughter

8. A Retirement

Dear Amma,

Today, as you retire, Amma,
I want to speak—not just as your child—
But as someone who watched, in awe,
As you lived many lives in one.

Papa is proud—
Not just of the wife who stood by him,
And of the woman who carved her name
In boardrooms and balance sheets.
And I—I'm proud to call you
My working mother.

I know you're proud too
When you look back at your journey—
But how easy was it, Amma?

How easy was it to be
A perfect wife and homemaker,
While adjusting to a new job?
To be an obedient daughter-in-law,
Who never forgot to pay the bills on time,
While still meeting deadlines,

Attending meetings,
And reaching your targets?

How easy was it to be
The best sister-in-law too—
Hosting celebration dinners,
Planning surprise cakes and late-night laughter
For others' wins,
While quietly wrestling
For your own promotion
In the chaos of office politics?

The ideal mother—
Who walked to work each day,
Carrying one question in her heart:
"Am I doing enough for my daughter?"

Yet every evening,
You were there—
Sitting beside me,
Helping with homework,
Listening to my school stories,
Like nothing else in the world mattered more.

You did it all, Amma—
Gracefully, powerfully, and silently.
You made it look effortless.

So today, I don't just say congratulations—
I say thank you.
For every unspoken sacrifice,
For every quiet strength,
For showing me what it means
To live with courage,
And to love without limits.

But Amma, is this really retirement?
Do you stop cooking?
Do you stop caring?
Do you stop managing our lives like you always have?
A mother never truly retires—
Her journey is eternal.

So rest—yes.
But know this:
Your work, your love, your legacy—
It continues in us.

Happy Retirement, Amma.

Forever yours,
Your daughter—your admirer.

9. Between Two Homes

Dear Amma,

This is my first letter to you
after my marriage.

I am happy here with your son-in-law—
life feels bright.
The days slip by so quickly,
I barely notice the seasons change.

This house is vast;
each room so spacious—
there's space for everyone.
Yet somehow, Amma,
I still can't stretch my legs
and feel at ease.
At times, it feels suffocating...
Did you ever feel the same?

No one here dislikes me.
Every day they ask gently,
"Are you comfortable?"
I am warmly welcomed to the dining table.

But Amma, I still ache for that heart-deep love—
the kind that needs no words, nor invitations.
Did you, too, long for it?

I'm not forced to wrap myself in sarees.
I'm free to wear jeans, salwars, midis...
and yet, I find myself waiting,
hoping to hear,
"You look beautiful."
Did you, too, wait like this?

The food here tastes better
than what I used to cook.
Yet every dish is called
too spicy or too bland.
I remember you eating my saltless upma,
smiling as if it were a feast.
Did you feel the same?

I'm never alone here.
There are people around me always.
I follow my husband wherever he goes—
but Amma...
why do I still feel lonely?
Did you, too, feel unseen
in those early days?

Amma, when will these strange feelings fade?
When will I start to feel loved... and at home?
When will I finally accept this as my home?
How long did it take for you, Ma?

Your daughter,
still learning to belong.

10. From Your Womb to My Heart

Dear Amma,

I'm so excited to tell you—
today, your grandbaby
kicked me from inside the womb.

I feel as if I'm in heaven,
wrapped in a sacred glow.

Those soft little kicks,
tiny bumpy limbs pressing gently...
Oh Amma,
what a miracle this feels like!

Tell me, Amma,
how did you feel
when I kicked you for the very first time?
What did you do then, Ma?

Did my tiny movements
fill you with a strange fullness?
A gentle ache in your belly,
as I swirled inside, restless and burpy.

Amma, did you ever get scared
when I slipped into silence,
forgetting to move
as you sang me lullabies?

Ma, how did you manage to walk,
so steadily, watching every step,
while I swam within you
and danced bhangra every time?

Amma, did I let you sleep?
Or was I kicking and playing all night—
even as you whispered bedtime stories,
knowing neither day nor night?

Now I understand, Ma—
this is more than just a kick.
It's the secret language of love,
spoken long before I opened my eyes.

**Your
mother-to-be daughter**

11. An Alive Daughter

Dear Amma,

You always say—
"I love you, dear.
Do what is right—both God and I are with you."
And you have stood true to your words.

When I hid my face in my hands and cried,
saying I could no longer bear
the beatings and scoldings from my husband—
you gently uncovered my face
and wiped away my tears.

When relatives said,
"What's so abusive? Every woman goes through this—
you're overreacting,"
you stood firm and said,
"Nobody has the right to raise a hand on my daughter."

When I walked back home after the divorce,
and people began to weave stories—
you stood beside me and said,
"An alive daughter is what I need,
not a dead one."

As I lay there,
having lost all hope and belief,
you gently breathed life back into my dreams
and encouraged me to follow my passion.
In doing so,
you gave me a rebirth.

You told me—
"Let your actions be louder than your words.
Be an inspiration to girls like you."

While sculpting me into who I am today,
you became my role model.

Your forever
grateful daughter.

12. The Godmother

Dear Amma,

Welcome back to motherhood.

As I walked home,
holding your grandchild after delivery,
I saw something new in you—
something timeless.

A mother—still dynamic—
who, though slowed by arthritis,
sat down without hesitation
to bathe your grandchild after a warm oil massage.

A mother who skipped her evening walk
with friends at the park,
just to sit beside me,
checking if I had taken my meds.

A mother who gave up her noon naps,
rocking the baby gently in her arms—
so I could close my eyes
and catch a little sleep.

A mother who forgot her own medicines,
but never missed a single vaccination date
for her little grandchild,
reading them aloud like sacred chants.

A mother who never cared for herself,
yet never once forgot to sterilize the feeding bottle,
and always checked the warmth of the milk
before placing it in tiny hands.

A mother who never thought of her own meals,
yet prepared every fruit and veggie purée
with utmost love and careful hands—
so her grandchild would never choke.

A mother who made me forget
that I, too, am now a mother—
because in your lap, Amma,
you cradled both me and my child.

I may be the mother of my child,
but I want him to know you
not just as a grandmother—
but as his **Godmother, Amma.**

Your little,
daughter—a new mom.

13. Amma's Telepathy

Dear Amma,

You are truly amazing—
but even more amazing
are your instincts, Amma.
You know me
before I know myself.

In the kitchen,
while stirring the curry,
you sense the silence—
a sudden pause—
I'm up to mischief.

At your office desk,
before the phone even rings,
you already know
my school will call—
I'm unwell.

In the market,
your hands reach for potatoes,
as if guided by magic—
to answer my craving
for hot, golden bajjias.

In the evening, lost
watching your favorite serial,
you pick the call at the first ring—
congratulating me
before I announce my promotion.

Far away,
in another country,
when I miss you deeply,
hiding my face under the pillow,
your video call rings—
to awaken my weary soul.

Amma,
you carry a map of me
within your heart—
and somehow,
you always know the way.

Thank you, Ma.
Your missing heartbeat.

14. The Man You Endured

Dear Amma,

As I pressed my ear against your door,
I heard you whisper secrets
to that tear-soaked pillow—
after Dad gifted you
those bruises on your neck.

I've watched you
murmur prayers to God,
begging for strength—
to endure the world's
most emotionless husband.

I've seen you
question your own worth,
drowning in self-doubt
after each gaslighting session
with Papa.

I've tiptoed and peeped
through the doorway,
as you held your nose and bent down—
cleaning vomit from the floor

after one of his fancy drunken parties.

And I've cried,
hearing you curse your fate,
trapped beside a man
who only ever loved himself—
a selfish monster.

I remained a silent witness.
I thought that was how life was meant to be—
until I understood
that the man in our life
was a master of mirrors,
a textbook narcissist.

Your daughter,
A silent spectator

15. The Secrets I Never Told

Dear Amma,

You've always been my best friend—
sometimes too strict,
sometimes wonderfully soft.
But there are secrets
I've carried quietly for years.
Today, I want to let them out.

As a little girl,
the secret behind my empty plate—
the dosas I slid beneath the sofa cushions,
and the milk I gently poured
into our puppy's eager mouth.

As a teenager,
though you laughed and shared
stories of your silly school crushes,
I kept mine locked away—
my maths teacher,
a quiet admiration
pressed like a flower between pages.

In college,

I bunked class for the first time,
slipping into a first-day, first-show movie,
my heart pounding louder
than the film's opening song.

When I began working,
I sipped wine with colleagues,
then whiskey too—
and woke the next morning
with a dizzy head
and a heart heavy with guilt.

As a married woman,
I cried softly into my pillow
when they asked me
to visit you less often,
to avoid staying overnight
in the home that raised me.

As a mother,
cradling a wailing baby at 3 a.m.,
I whispered into the darkness:
"Do I even want to be a mother?
Was life simpler when I was alone?"

All these truths, Amma—
I hid them not out of fear,
but because they felt too heavy then,
too raw to share.
Now, as I grow older,
they almost seem... tenderly silly.

So today I've poured out
every secret—whether small or shocking—
because I know
you will never judge me.
You will only gather me
into your arms,
the way you always have.

Your
secret-keeping daughter

16. Bridging Generations

Dear Amma,

You told me, "Respect your elders."
I replied, "Respect is only for the deserving."

You told me, "Sharing is caring."
I replied, "It only makes me taken for granted."

You told me, "Never give back answers."
I replied, "But questioning is a skill."

You told me, "Adjustment is life."
I replied, "It's freedom to set boundaries."

You told me, "Cooking and cleaning are a must for a girl."
I replied, "Life skills shouldn't be gender-biased."

You told me, "Modernization has swept away our
traditions and culture."
I replied, "It's not modernization, Amma—it's science,
and we need to move with change."

I said, "Your teachings are the foundation—
some are meant to be learned,
and some to be unlearned."

You replied, "Then build yours upon that,
but make sure it grows strong—
and does not collapse."

Your
Millennial Daughter

17. The Light You Gave Me

Dear Amma,

Today, as I walked through the door
Of the house where I once played and ran,
Something felt different—strangely unfamiliar.

Everyone welcomed me... but with pity.
Everyone—except you.

You opened your arms to your widow daughter,
Not with sympathy,
But with the same love and warmth
With which you held me
When I came home from school,
Exhausted after a long, grueling sports day.

I was a living corpse,
No strength left to lift my soul.
Though you, too, had walked beside me
Through this journey of loss and grief,
You never let it show.

You held me with courage,
Even as your heart quietly broke.
There were days I wished
My life had ended with his...

I wanted to shut the doors
And stay behind in that darkness.
Though drowning in the same sorrow,
You held the guiding lamp—
Showing me the meaning of life.

You swallowed your tears
And wiped away mine,
Holding me up,
Helping me rise again—
Not as a widow,
But as a mother
Standing tall for her child.

Amma,
You didn't just welcome me home—
You brought me back to life.

Your
strong daughter

18. The Bandit Mother

Dear Amma,

Born in an era when untouchable
was a brand seared into the skin,
into a home where poverty
stole every trace of joy
before it could bloom.

Not long after, you stood
beside a stranger—an elderly groom—
as his wife, though you looked
more like his grandchild,
a child bride in borrowed bangles.

Too soon, you became a young mother,
worn down by an abusive husband—
a drunkard who even pawned
his own wife for a few annas,
trading dignity for drink.

You fought back in that brothel,
clinging fiercely to chastity's edge,
then fled and found shelter
among the dacoits—
becoming the Robin Hood of the ravines.

You struck back at Thakurs who preyed
on women, mocking the weak.
You feared none, standing alone
for the justice denied to many—
wronged in the name of caste and status.

At last, you surrendered to the law,
enduring long trials and years behind bars.
You emerged with dignity, unbroken,
rising as a minister from the suppressed—
the voice of the voiceless in the House.

Your story filled the headlines,
your good deeds echoing far
across the dust of forgotten lands.
But soon, you fell to an assassin's bullet—
a bold voice silenced too soon.

You not only adopted me, Ma,
but a whole village of the forgotten.
You carved a path we still follow—

a saint born of suffering's flame.
Here, you are remembered,
worshipped as the Mother God.

Your loving
Child of the Forgotten Land

Phoolan Devi (1963–2001), known as the "Bandit Queen"
of Chambal, rose from a life of oppression and violence
to become a Member of Parliament in India. Her journey
—from child bride and outlaw leader to political icon—
remains a powerful symbol of resilience, justice, and
defiance against systemic injustice.

19. Letter from the Ashes

Dear Amma,

From my heavenly abode,
I see you every day.
I see you weeping endlessly,
drowning in the memories of me.

My cries held no worth that night—
on those dark, merciless streets—
as the ravens tore at every inch
of my body and my soul.

When they were done,
they flung me to the road—
stripped of every shred of dignity—
not a single cloth to cover me.

When you saw me on the hospital bed—
bleeding, broken,
torn into pieces by demons
wearing street-dog masks—

you collapsed in grief,
your heart unable to hold
the horror of my wounds
and the cruelty of the world.

The so-called elites
spoke in media houses,
ripping me apart every hour,
turning my agony into headlines.

When my torn body was buried,
justice was buried with it—
under hollow, shameless tags:
"minor," "mentally unsound," "politically sensitive."

Who cares for a girl
in this cruel, material world?
Only you, Amma, fought
with your whole being for me.

And from here,
I burn with fury—
for being born in a land
that still shields the guilty.

But Amma... do not stop.
Let my ashes fly through your words,
let my silence scream in your fight—
until no daughter joins me this way.

Your justice-denied
Daughter

This poem is written in remembrance of victims like
Nirbhaya,Dr. Moumita Debnath and Soujanya.
It is dedicated to every daughter whose voice was
silenced by violence,and whose justice remains buried
under bureaucracy, prejudice, and power.
May their ashes speak through us—
until no mother weeps alone

20. Conversation Over Coffee

Dear Amma,

A strong, freshly brewed coffee—
dark as midnight,
filled right to the brim,
its surface freckled with trembling bubbles.

Outside, the sky shifted from crimson to blue,
while birds stitched the sky home.

It felt like an evening made for light talk.

"Sita," I said, "epitome of sacrifice—
she had it all: beautiful, brave, gentle,
a single mother."

You nodded, then said with quiet force:
"Never keep silent and agree to all.
Learn to speak when needed.
Never make sacrifices that mean nothing.
Love is not all about sacrifice—
self-love is just as important."

A pause lingered before my next words:

"Gandhari—princess of Gandhara,
devoted wife, mother of the Kauravas—
again, a symbol of selfless sacrifice."

Your eyes held mine as you said:
"Don't blindfold yourself to the truth.
See right from wrong, and when wrong stands before
you,
find the courage to question it.
Otherwise, your sacrifice becomes a shield for the
wrongdoers."

I sipped my coffee before speaking again:

"Draupadi—the innocent one,
a rejected daughter once,
and later, Panchali, wife of five."

You leaned in, voice firm and warm:
"Don't stand helpless.
When the moment calls for it, fight back.
Do not wait for saviors to arrive—
the strength you seek is already yours.
Krishna is within you,
guiding your hand & arming your heart."

The last sip of coffee gone,
the evening grew still, yet stronger in spirit.
The sun disappeared beyond the horizon,
leaving behind its afterglow—
and your words, glowing brighter than dusk.

Your
wisdom-seeking daughter

21. My Annapoorneshwari

Dear Amma,

As I stood in the kitchen today—
an amateur cook with uncertain hands—
I found myself thinking of you,
and the quiet magic you weave.

Without a single measuring spoon,
you know—without a thermometer—
when the water is just hot enough
for the perfect coffee decoction.

How do you know so precisely
when to turn off the cooker—
two whistles for rice, five for dal—
not a whistle more, nor a moment late?

How do you sense the salt—
just enough for savor,
subtle enough for sweetness,
never tipping over to spike the sugar?

How do you know when the oil
is perfectly hot—ready to bloom
the fryums into golden, crispy delight—
without smoke, without fuss?

How do you cook the perfect chicken—
rich broth, tender and juicy meat—
never overdone, never raw—
a skill that feels like silent wisdom?

And when a dish doesn't turn out right,
you mend it like magic—quietly,
skillfully—so we never go to sleep
with hunger in our hearts.

You are the master chef, Amma,
with a secret ingredient in every dish—
a charm that goes beyond taste,
a warmth that goes beyond words.

It is your immense love
that you add so lavishly—
in every stir, every spice,
and every gentle spoonful.

You are my Annapoorneshwari—
the goddess who feeds heart and soul.
More than just food on a plate,
you make our lives feel whole.

Forever your
Grateful daughter

22. Oh Amma

Oh Amma, I write to you with pride and worry,
for you are vast—sheltering millions upon millions.

Oh Amma, shielded by mountains that kiss the clouds,
and oceans that stretch without end.

Oh Amma, evergreen, with forests that breathe life into
the air,
and cities rising as towering concrete jungles.

Oh Amma, rich, with veins of gold, iron, and diamond,
and rivers flowing with your children's talent.

Oh Amma, adorned with the grace of dancers,
the song of musicians, and the art of dreamers.

Oh Amma, brilliant, with the wisdom of sages,
the guidance of teachers, and the vision of scientists.

Oh Amma, the cradle of civilizations and revolutions,
a treasure of cultures and traditions older than time.

Oh Amma, fearless, who shattered the chains of slavery
by walking the path of ahimsa.

Oh Amma, now slowly losing your democracy
to the glitter of capitalism, wrapped in soft silk of
privatization.

Oh Amma, guard the freedom you bled to win,
for you were born to shape your fate—never to be ruled.

Your
devoted children

*Oh Amma is a love letter to Mother India—her beauty,
courage, and spirit. Written from the hearts of her
children, it celebrates her bounty and wisdom while
urging care and protection for the challenges she faces in
a changing world.*